IMAGES
of America

PORT ORANGE

Port Orange Historical Trust Officers
Harold D. Cardwell Sr., president
Christine Doughty, vice president
Thelma Cardwell, secretary
Carol Kubacki, treasurer

Port Orange School Reunion Committee
Glenda Coursen, chairman
Christine Doughty
Barbara Kazebeer
Thelma Cardwell

Port Orange City Government
Dorothy L. Hukill, mayor
Dan Eddy, vice mayor
Kenneth W. Parker, city manager
William R. Whitson, assistant city manager
Clifford "Buzzy" Windle, council member
Mary Martin, council member
John Jackson, council member

IMAGES of America
PORT ORANGE

Harold D. Cardwell Sr. and Priscilla D. Cardwell

ARCADIA PUBLISHING

Copyright © 2000 by Harold D. Cardwell Sr. and Priscilla D. Cardwell
ISBN 9781531603953

Published by Arcadia Publishing
Charleston, South Carolina

Library of Congress Catalog Card Number: 00-105911

For all general information contact Arcadia Publishing at:
Telephone 843-853-2070
Fax 843-853-0044
E-mail sales@arcadiapublishing.com
For customer service and orders:
Toll-Free 1-888-313-2665

Visit us on the Internet at www.arcadiapublishing.com

This book is dedicated to all the members of the Port Orange Historical Trust, who had the vision to organize a trust that would preserve our history and manage our heritage resources for the future.

ABOUT THE AUTHORS

Harold D. Cardwell Sr. is a retired Senior Rehabilitation Specialist with the Florida Department of Labor and Employment Security, Division of Blind Services. He is a registered landscape architect and horticultural therapist (emeritus) and a lifelong resident of Volusia County. He is a graduate of Florida Technological University. During World War II, he was assigned to the Atomic Bomb Project at Oak Ridge, Tennessee, and Los Alamos, New Mexico. Mr. Cardwell is currently chairman of the Daytona Beach Historic Preservation Board, president of the Port Orange Historical Trust, and active in many other state historical organizations.

Priscilla D. Cardwell is a lifelong resident of Volusia County. She worked for Volusia County Human Services for 22 years as a social worker, retiring in 1997. A graduate of Florida Technological University, she is currently a member of the Volusia County Historic Preservation Board, the Halifax Historical Society, the Port Orange Historical Trust, the Volusia Anthropological Society, the Florida Historical Society, and the Florida Historic Trust.

Contents

Acknowledgments 6

Bibliography 6

Introduction 7

1. Prehistoric Times 9

2. Europeans and the Territorial Period 19

3. Statehood, Civil War, and Post Civil War 33

4. Transportation and Early Industry 43

5. Cultural Changes 57

6. World War I and the Land Boom 69

7. The Great Depression 83

8. World War II and Post War 97

9. Growth and the Future 115

Acknowledgments

Thanks go to the following individuals and organizations:

The Port Orange Historical Trust, Museum and Archives; the Halifax Historical Museum; the Florida State Library and State Archives; the St. Augustine Historical Society Library; the Cardwell Family Collection; Diane M. Bara; William DuBois; Russell Smith; Roy Midkiff; Shirley Sheppard; Don Serbousek; Carol Kubacki; Wilbur Haller; Rufus Jackson; John Gontner; the Archives of the Port Orange Historical Trust; the State of Florida; the St. Augustine Historical Society; the Halifax Historical Society; the News-Journal Corporation; Cardwell Family Collection, 1976.

Bibliography

Adams, William R., Ph.D. *Historic Properties Survey of Port Orange, Florida*. St. Augustine: Historic Property Associates, Inc., 1996.

Bathe, Greville. *Engineer's Notebook*. St. Augustine: St. Augustine Record Press, 1955.

Dau, Frederick W. *Florida—Old and New*. Detroit: Gale Research Company, 1975.

Fitzgerald, T.E. *Volusia County: Past and Present*. Daytona Beach: The Observer Press, 1937.

Gold, Pleasant Daniel. *History of Volusia County, Florida*. Deland, FL: The E.O. Painter Printing Company, 1927.

Hawks, John M. *The East Coast of Florida*. Lynn, MA: Lewis and Winship, 1887.

Hebel, Ianthe B. *Centennial History of Volusia County, Florida, 1854–1954*. Daytona Beach: College Publishing Company, 1955.

Knetsch, Joseph, Ph.D. "The Battle of Dunlawton." *Halifax Herald*. Port Orange, FL: Lithocraft Inc., 1998.

Schene, Michael G. *Hopes, Dreams, and Promises: A History of Volusia County, Florida*. Daytona Beach: News-Journal Corporation, 1976.

INTRODUCTION

This history will take you back 130,000 years, during the Pleistocene Period, when there were a number of prehistoric animals in our vicinity. The Nova bone-bed, south of Reed Canal Road, and at least two other bone-beds within the boundaries of Port Orange, have yielded the skeletal remains of the Giant Ground Sloth, Mastodon, Mammoth, Bison, Sabre-toothed cat, and the geological aspects of their environment.

Archeological research has revealed that man was in the Port Orange area approximately 7,000 years ago. Environmental changes provided conditions for abundant food resources, which enabled early man to survive and establish temporary camps along the east coast. Early man continued to migrate throughout the centuries to the Spruce Creek and Halifax River region. Evidence of their habitation is exhibited by the projectile points, pot shards, and other artifacts found in the Spruce Creek Mound and at Green Mound.

The prehistoric period ended upon the arrival of the Europeans in the 16th century. Cultural changes and diseases resulted in the extinction of the Timucuan culture. Prior to the demise of the Timucuans, the Seminoles started their migration into the area.

Juan Ponce de Leon arrived in this region in 1513 and, in the name of the king of Spain, claimed this land, which he named Florida. After more than 200 years, Spain ceded the Florida territory to England in 1763 at the Treaty of Paris. During the English Period, Dr. Andrew Turnbull received a grant of land and established a colony at New Smyrna. The boundaries of this plantation extended into the southern portion of the City of Port Orange today. The English re-ceded the Florida territory to Spain, in return for the Bahamas and other lands, at the Second Treaty of Paris in 1783.

In 1804 Patrick Dean arrived in the Port Orange area from the Bahamas and established a plantation to grow indigo, cotton, rice, and sugar cane, which were cultivated by slaves. Apparently he met his fate at the hands of a renegade Indian during the First Indian War in 1818.

The Dunlawton Sugar Mill was established in 1832 on 995 acres previously owned by Patrick Dean. A broker sold the old Dean Plantation to Sarah Anderson and her two sons, George and James. The name Dunlawton was derived from her maiden name, Dunn, and the land dealer's name, Lawton. The mill was operated by slave labor until the fall of 1835.

The Second Seminole Indian War started in December 1835 with skirmishes at Fort King and New Smyrna, and the Dade Massacre and the Battle of Dunlawton. The conflict continued pushing the Seminoles further south, with the war finally ending in 1842.

Statehood came in 1845 and shortly afterwards settlers started to arrive in the area. John Marshall, a planter from Louisiana, bought the Dunlawton Plantation in 1847. However, after a few years, Dunlawton failed, once again, because of the marketing of sugar, the high cost of slaves, and the Civil War. The Dunlawton Mill fell into disrepair and only the kettles were used for salt production near the end of the Civil War.

In 1865–1866, Dr. John Milton Hawks, a Union Army surgeon, brought 500 freed slaves and their families to this area. The colony soon failed and most fled the area to return to former plantations in Georgia and South Carolina. However, some did stay and found work in the citrus and timber enterprises. Dr. Hawks named the area Port Orange in 1867.

In 1871, John Marshall sold the Dunlawton Plantation to William Dougherty and his son Charles. Charles inherited this plantation when his father died unexpectedly. However, he was a lawyer and politician and had no skills in agriculture. The mill never operated again.

In the 1880s, land speculators began arriving in the Port Orange area, at which time large citrus groves were planted and the timber industry prospered. Henry Flagler extended the Florida East Coast Railroad to Port Orange in 1892 and brought about a new industry called tourism. Accommodations for tourists were built along the riverfront, and the train depot was completed in 1894. The big freeze of 1894–1895 wiped out the inland groves. Fortunately, the tourism and fishing industries saved the growing community. A town hall was built, as well as the first Port Orange School in 1889.

After the turn of the century, roads were developed for the horse and carriage and later improved for the automobile. The citrus industry again enjoyed many years of growth without disastrous freezes, and the Port Orange Bridge was built in 1906.

Port Orange became a town in 1913 with Dr. Henry Du Bois as mayor. The cattle industry became more dominant in the years prior to World War I. Following WW I, the town of Port Orange grew to become a city in 1925—utilities became available and tourist accommodations dotting the landscape. Also at this time a new Port Orange School was completed.

Then came the Great Depression, as well as the demise of the Port Orange Bridge in 1932. During this period the population was less than 1,000. WW II put Port Orange back on the map with the building of the United States Navy Auxiliary Landing Field. Port Orange grew slowly until the completion of the second Port Orange Bridge in 1951.

By the 1970s and 1980s, Port Orange experienced significant population growth. In the 1990s, there were many new schools, churches, shopping centers, and prestigious subdivisions. Although largely a bedroom community, it is believed that the Port Orange population will expand to 50,000 by 2001.

This short pictorial history has been compiled in an effort to preserve our past and as a way to help citizens of the future manage our historic heritage resources.

One

PREHISTORIC TIMES

REED CANAL LAKE, WHERE GIANT GROUND SLOTH REMAINS WERE DISCOVERED, 1975–1978. There were many partial remains of the Giant Ground Sloth, Mastodon, Mammoth, Horse, and many smaller animals of the Pleistocene Period excavated in this bone bed. Dr. Gordon Edmund and the Royal Ontario Museum, Toronto, Canada, have a similar Giant Ground Sloth on display that also came from this bone bed. The missing bone(s) were replaced with molded fiberglass replicas (i.e. ribs, etc.). This discovery provided an almost complete skeleton for both the Daytona and Toronto Museums. (Courtesy of Don Serbousek.)

SITE WHERE THE GIANT GROUND SLOTH WAS FOUND. This marker gives details of the sloth and the area. (Courtesy of Don Serbousek.)

GIANT GROUND SLOTH (EREMOTHERIUM MIRABILI) AND ITS DISCOVERERS, MUSEUM OF ARTS AND SCIENCES, DAYTONA BEACH, 1975–1978. From left to right are Steve Hartman, Dr. Gordon Edmund, Roger Alexon, and Don Serbousek. Dr. Edmund, a world recognized specialist in Ground Sloths, revealed through pollen dating that this animal was 130,000 years old. The skeleton material of this animal was excavated from the Nova Bone Bed near Port Orange. (Courtesy of Don Serbousek.)

PREHISTORIC GIANT GROUND SLOTH, A MOLDED CONCRETE REPLICA AT THE SUGAR MILL BOTANICAL GARDENS. This was once a planned zoological exhibit for "Bongoland"—a tourist attraction that failed in the 1950s. (Courtesy of Port Orange Historical Trust.)

DUNLAWTON SUGAR MILL GARDENS, PORT ORANGE, FLORIDA, 1959. This is a Triceratops, part of a zoological exhibit at Bongoland. (Courtesy of Florida State Archives.)

DIMETRODON. The prehistoric replicas on display throughout the garden area of Dunlawton Sugar Mill Botanical Gardens were originally planned as part of a zoological exhibit. Today they remain at strategic points along the nature trail. (Courtesy Port Orange Historical Trust.)

BONGOLAND EXHIBIT, 1959. The concrete casts of these prehistoric animals are very popular with visitors at the Dunlawton Sugar Mill Gardens. These are life-size replicas of (left) Stegosaurus and (right) Tyranosaurus Rex. (Courtesy of Florida State Archives.

SUGAR MILL BOTANICAL GARDENS, 1959. Unidentified children gaze at the replica of Tyranosaurus Rex. Bongoland is no more; however, the prehistoric animals remain on display today throughout the gardens. (Courtesy of Florida State Archives.)

SUGAR MILL BOTANICAL GARDENS, 1959. Unidentified children are pictured sitting on top of Stegosaurus. Children are always excited by the presence of the prehistoric animal sculptures located at the gardens. (Courtesy of Florida State Archives.)

DUNLAWTON SUGAR MILL GARDENS, PORT ORANGE, FLORIDA, 1959. This dinosaur statue was part of a zoological section of the former Bongoland. An unidentified child sits on top of the Stegosaurus sculpture. (Courtesy of Florida State Archives.)

FERN GROTTO AT THE VOLUSIA COUNTY BOTANICAL GARDENS, PORT ORANGE, FLORIDA. These species are propagated from spores placed in crevasses on the stone wall. (Courtesy of Port Orange Historical Trust.)

PREHISTORIC SHELL MOUNDS, ALLANDALE, FLORIDA. There were several mounds at Spruce Creek and middens to the north of Port Orange. There were also several Timucuan villages on Spruce Creek and the Halifax River in Port Orange. (Courtesy of Port Orange Historical Trust.)

TIMUCUAN FORTIFIED VILLAGE, 1562. Today, archaeological sites yield cultural material that verifies the early existence of these natives. (Courtesy of Florida State Archives.)

TIMUCUAN INDIANS GOING OFF TO WAR, 1562. Several Native American villages once existed along Spruce Creek and the northern edge of Port Orange. (Courtesy of Florida State Archives.)

PREHISTORIC INDIAN MOUND. Harold Cardwell surveys one of the many Indian mounds and middens along the Halifax River in Volusia County, Florida. (Courtesy of Cardwell Family Collection.)

FLORIDA WARRIOR CHIEF. An early rendering shows tribal warriors performing their warring or ritual activities. Middens and mounds, showing signs of early Native American habitation, are located along Spruce Creek and the Halifax River. (Courtesy of Florida State Archives.)

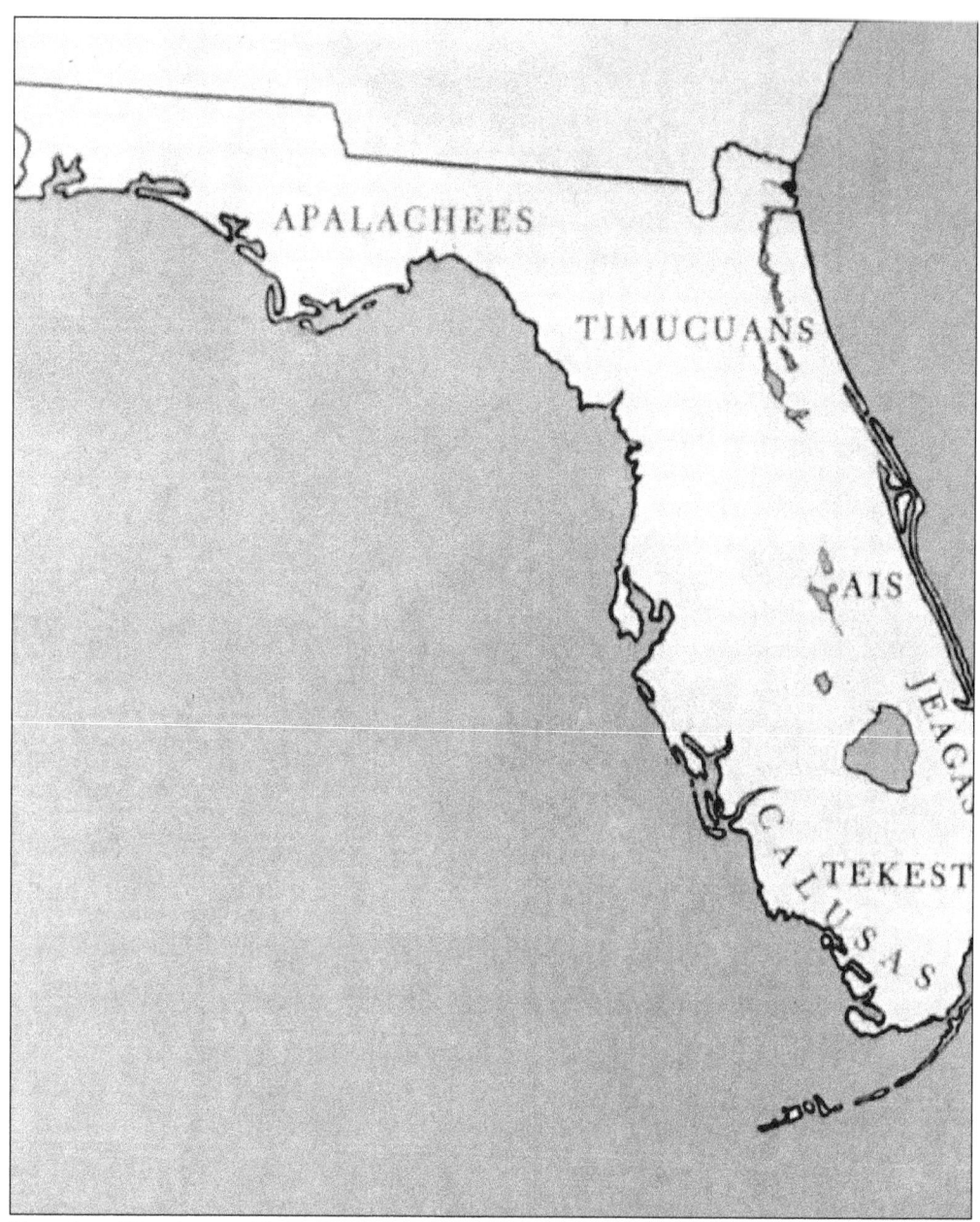

THE AIS. The Ais, and later Timucuan, Indian tribes are indicated on the map where Port Orange is located today. These were aboriginal tribes, both pre-historic and historic. (Courtesy of Florida State Archives.)

Two

EUROPEANS AND THE TERRITORIAL PERIOD

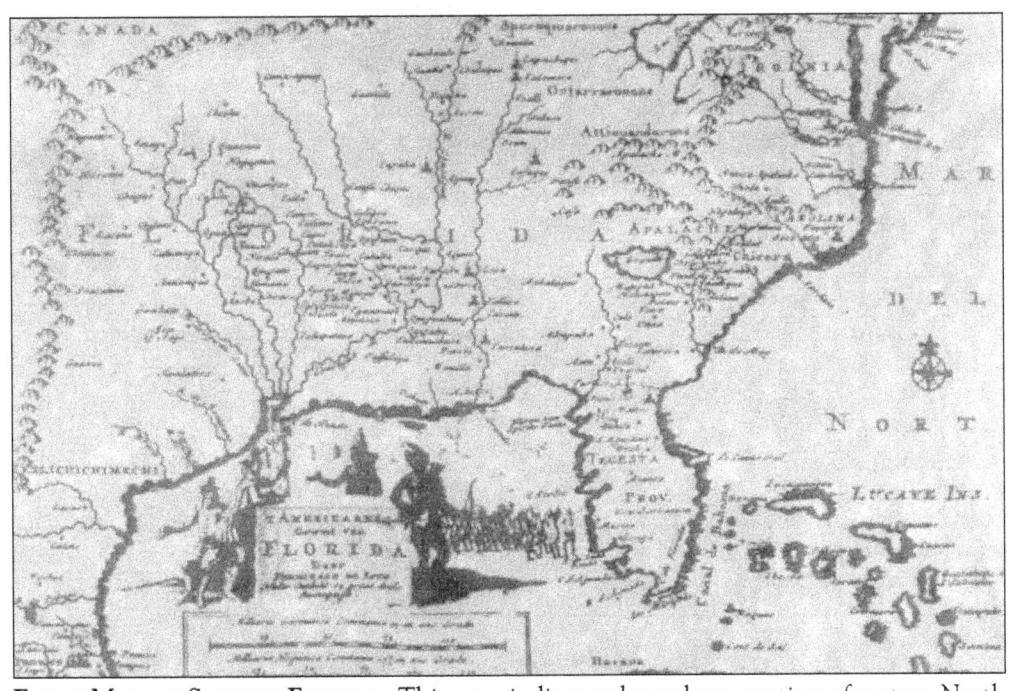

EARLY MAP OF SPANISH FLORIDA. This map indicates that a large portion of eastern North America was Florida. (Courtesy of Port Orange Historical Trust.)

JUAN PONCE DE LEON. In the spring of 1513, Juan Ponce de Leon sailed along the Atlantic coast of what is now Volusia County. Some historians believe he landed at the inlet that now bears his name. The river, which he called De la Cruz ("River of the Cross"), was at the confluence of Spruce Creek, the Halifax and Indian Rivers north. Ponce de Leon named this territory "Florida" after the beautiful flora he saw on his journey. (Courtesy of Florida State Archives.)

GOVERNOR JAMES GRANT. Grant was the first British governor of the Territory of Florida during the English period, 1763–1783. (Courtesy of Halifax Historical Society.)

JOHN MOULTRIE. Moultrie was the first lieutenant governor of Florida during the English Period, 1763–1783. (Courtesy of Halifax Historical Society.)

DR. ANDREW TURNBULL. Turnbull established a colony at New Smyrna in 1767. The official land grant issued to Turnbull on June 18, 1766, allowed him to select a tract of 20,000 acres and no more than 30 square miles of unclaimed land on the east coast of Florida. The northern line of his English grant ran east and west through the present-day City of Port Orange. (Courtesy of Florida State Archives.)

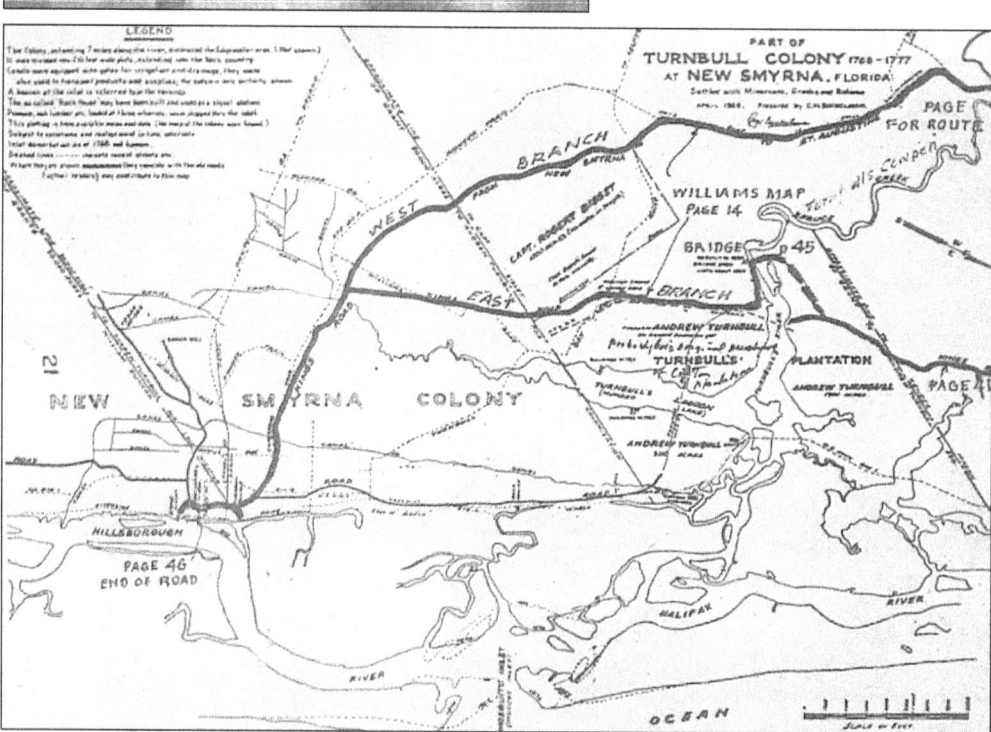

MAP OF THE TURNBULL COLONY, 1768–1777. This map shows the northern boundary of the colony, which lies inside the southern boundary of the City of Port Orange. (Courtesy of Halifax Historical Society.)

PATRICK TONYN, ENGLISH TERRITORIAL GOVERNOR, 1774. Tonyn and Turnbull were continually at odds over the declining conditions of the plantation at New Smyrna. The volatile situation between the territorial governor and Turnbull hastened the demise of the Turnbull Colony. The English recession of the Florida Territory to Spain in 1783 affected the land boundaries that eventually became the City of Port Orange. (Courtesy of Florida State Archives.)

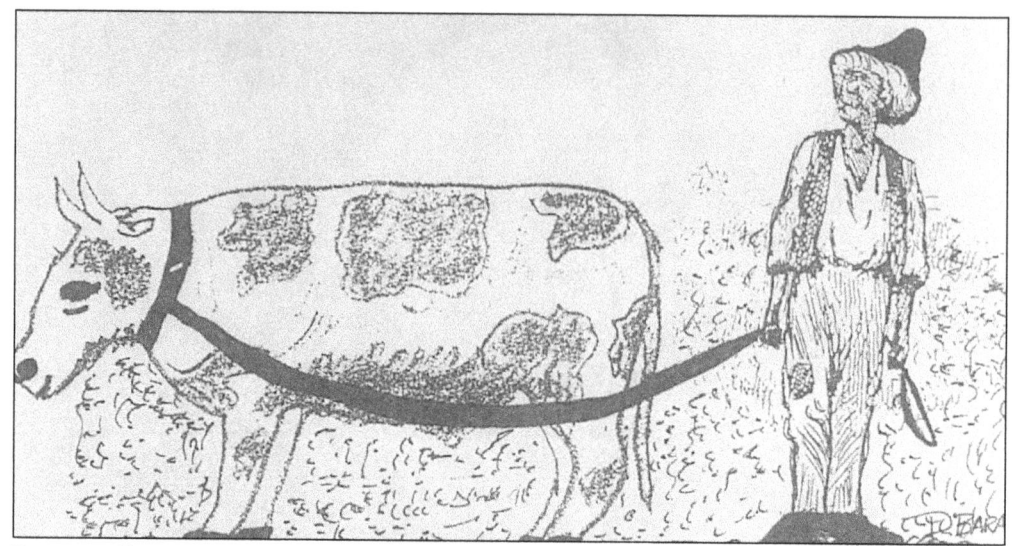

PATRICK DEAN AND HIS RELIABLE OX (ARTIST'S RENDERING). Dean established his plantation in 1804 on 995 acres granted by the Spanish crown. The primary crops were rice, cotton, indigo, and sugar cane. His mill was animal drawn, and the crops were cultivated and harvested by slaves. It was located in the Mosquitoes, which is today the City of Port Orange. (Courtesy of Diane M. Bara.)

SAMUEL WILLIAMS PLANTATION AND ITS CANE CRUSHER ON THE GROUNDS OF THE SUGAR MILL BOTANICAL GARDENS. This is the only physical remains of the Williams Plantation. The photo was taken in 1999. (Courtesy of Cardwell Family Collection.)

DUNLAWTON PLANTATION RUINS, PORT ORANGE, FLORIDA, C. 1920. This was an ox-cart road that ran between the cane crusher and mill house. Sugar cane was unloaded here for processing. This mill operated from 1832 until the Second Seminole Indian War began in December 1835. (Courtesy of Florida State Archives.)

DUNLAWTON SUGAR MILL GARDENS, 1946. Estelle Brock stands beside the cane crusher rollers of the old sugar mill ruins. In 1999, this machinery was realigned and placed on new bed-timbers. (Courtesy of Florida State Archives.)

DUNLAWTON SUGAR MILL MACHINERY. These parts were excavated on site in 1980. The mill operated from 1832 to 1835. (Courtesy of Port Orange Historical Trust.)

DUNLAWTON SUGAR MILL. This photo shows a fly wheel, crusher, and boiler—machinery restored by Volusia County and the State of Florida Comprehensive Educational Training Act Grant Program. The photo was taken in 1981. (Courtesy of Cardwell Family Collection.)

MEMBERS OF THE FLORIDA TRUST, ATTENDING THE COQUINA STONE CONFERENCE, JANUARY 2000. The members are shown touring the restored area of the Dunlawton Sugar Mill in Port Orange. This hand-cut coquina was quarried 168 years ago. (Courtesy of Port Orange Historical Trust.)

PURGING VATS AT SUGAR MILL BOTANICAL GARDENS. In 1834, cross-timbers held barrels that dripped the sugar syrup into these vats. The syrup was eventually sold as molasses. (Courtesy of Port Orange Historical Trust.)

BRIG. GEN. JOSEPH M. HERNANDEZ, LAWYER, MILITARY OFFICER, AND PLANTATION OWNER. During the Second Seminole Indian War, Hernandez was in command of the state militia and, later, the United States Army headquartered at St. Augustine. Two skirmishes took place on the Dunlawton Plantation during this period under his command. (Courtesy of Florida State Archives.)

HISTORIC MARKER FOR THE BATTLE OF DUNLAWTON PLANTATION. After losing this battle, General Joseph Hernandez and Major Benjamin Putnam were alarmed at the immediate danger of other plantations, including the town of St. Augustine on the east coast of Florida. (Courtesy of Port Orange Historical Trust.)

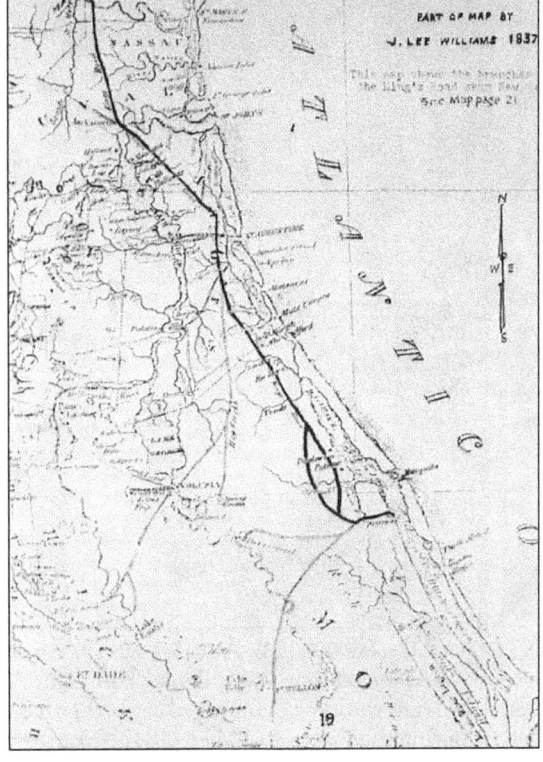

A MAP BY J. LEE WILLIAMS, 1837. The portion of the map shown here depicts the branches of King's Road near Port Orange. (Courtesy of Halifax Historical Society.)

HOME OF SARAH ANDERSON, ST. AUGUSTINE, FLORIDA. Sarah and her two sons, George and James, established a plantation in 1832 and named it Dunlawton. This name was a combination of her maiden name, Dunn, and the previous owner, named Lawton, a land dealer and merchant from Charleston, South Carolina. To this day the name still stands. After the end of the Second Seminole Indian War, this plantation was sold to John Marshall, a planter from Louisiana. Sarah Anderson lived out her days in St. Augustine and operated an inn at her home, pictured here, until her death. (Courtesy of Port Orange Historical Trust.)

NATIONAL CEMETERY, ST. AUGUSTINE. Pictured are pyramids of the fallen soldiers of the Indian Wars, including those fallen at Fort Dade. The men that died from their wounds at the Battle of Dunlawton are entombed with their comrades, who died in various skirmishes and battles during the war from 1835 to 1842. (Courtesy of Port Orange Historical Trust.)

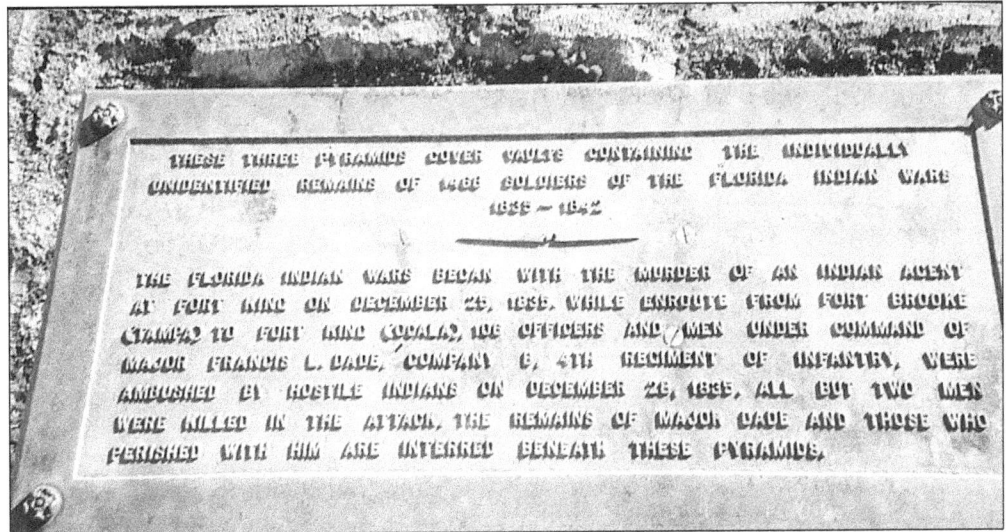

THREE PYRAMIDS' MARKER. The marker shows Major Dade, his men, and other soldiers who were killed during the Florida Indian Wars. (Courtesy of National Cemetery, St. Augustine.)

ARTIST'S RENDERING OF SEMINOLE WARS. In the fall of 1835 on the Dunlawton Plantation, George and James Anderson were constructing a "Bulwark" fortification. When the military call to duty came, they were forced to abandon their efforts and join the Florida militia to protect all plantations south of St. Augustine, along the east coast of Florida. (Courtesy of Florida State Archives.)

JOHN BRANCH, THE LAST UNITED STATES TERRITORIAL GOVERNOR OF FLORIDA. Branch assisted in the cause of bringing the Florida Territory into statehood in 1845. At this time, our area was called Dunlawton, and previous to 1832, it was called the Mosquitoes. Today, we call our town Port Orange. (Courtesy of Florida State Archives.)

Three

STATEHOOD, CIVIL WAR, AND POST CIVIL WAR

FLORIDA STATE SEAL. Florida gained statehood in 1845. (Courtesy of Florida State Archives.)

VOLUSIA COUNTY BOTANICAL GARDENS. The gardens are located in the old Dunlawton Plantation–Hammock area. This trail features many varieties of trees, including sweet gum, oak, ash, magnolia, and sabal palms. (Courtesy of Port Orange Historical Trust.)

JOHN MARSHALL'S SAW AND GRIST MILL ARCHEOLOGICAL RUINS. This mill operated in the 1850s and was located on the Dunlawton Plantation near the Halifax River. It is pictured here in 1981. (Courtesy of Cardwell Family Collection.)

DUNLAWTON PLANTATION, SUGAR HOUSE AND MILL, 950 OLD SUGAR MILL ROAD, C. 1870S. The ruins of this mill are located on the Patrick Dean Grant, 1804, which contained 995 acres of land. George and James Anderson built this plantation, and it was almost completely destroyed during the Second Seminole Indian War (1835–1842). Later, John Marshall rebuilt and restored this plantation around 1849. This mill was last operated in 1856. (Courtesy of Port Orange Historical Trust.)

CONFEDERATE OAK, SUGAR MILL BOTANICAL GARDENS. During the Civil War, Confederate soldiers (St. John's Rangers) on reconnaissance duty camped in the millhouse and hitched their horses near this tree. From this site they continued their expedition to New Smyrna and Enterprise. (Courtesy of Port Orange Historical Trust.)

SUGAR MILL FIREBOXES. In the foreground are the fireboxes once used to heat the kettles for the production of sugar (1832–1835), salt (1864–1865), and for rendering whale oil, a trial project that failed in 1906. Notice the beautiful brick construction. (Courtesy of Port Orange Historical Trust.)

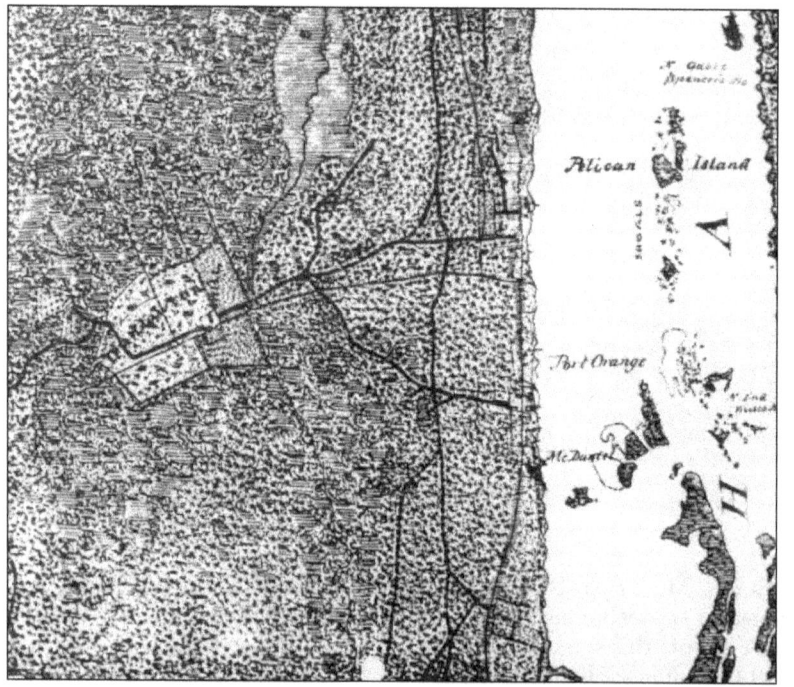

DUNLAWTON PLANTATION, AFTER THE CIVIL WAR. Notice the corduroy roads (built-up roads with cross logs and soil) connecting the other roads through the plantation. Pelican Island and the McDaniel site on the river are also visible. (Courtesy of Port Orange Historical Trust.)

CHARLES DOUGHERTY (LEFT) AND WILLIAM JACKSON (RIGHT), C. 1880S. Charles Dougherty, a local lawyer, was elected to the Florida Assembly in 1877; as speaker of the Florida House of Representatives in 1881 and 1883; to the United States House of Representatives from 1885 to 1889; to the Florida House of Representatives in 1891; to the Florida Senate in 1895 and 1897; and to the Florida House of Representatives again in 1911. Dougherty owned the Dunlawton Plantation in Port Orange for many years. William Jackson was a local merchant and a Daytona city councilman, and was very influential in politics in Volusia County. Jackson's first store, behind the Palmetto House, was the site of the incorporation of Daytona. His second store was located in Port Orange for a short period of time before returning to Daytona. (Courtesy of Halifax Historical Society.)

DR. J.M. HAWKS. Hawks was a Union Army officer and surgeon during the Civil War. After the war ended, he set out from Fort Royal, South Carolina, in 1865–1866, to establish a colony. He brought 500 freedmen and their families to this area and established the Florida Land and Lumber Company. However, both the colony and the company failed. Some freedmen stayed, while others made their way back to their original home places throughout the South. Dr. Hawks is credited with naming the town Port Orange in 1867. (Courtesy of Halifax Historical Society.)

RIVERVIEW HOTEL. The hotel was built c. 1872 on the west bank of the Halifax River. This view shows the northwest corner of Halifax Drive and Dunlawton Avenue in 1997. Over the years the building was operated as a hotel, a sanitarium, and, for the last few years, as apartments. Other names associated with the building were Grandview Sanitarium, Alligator Inn, and Riverside Apartments. (Courtesy of Port Orange Historical Trust.)

RIVERSIDE INN ON THE CORNER OF HALIFAX DRIVE AND DUNLAWTON AVENUE, PORT ORANGE. The inn was originally built in 1872, and there were many renovations over the years. In the early days, tourists would arrive by train and passengers would be transported from the train depot to the inn by horse and carriage. This view of the hotel was taken in 1986. (Courtesy of Port Orange Historical Trust.)

BRYAN HOME, BUILT C. 1886, OFF WEST HERBERT STREET, PORT ORANGE. Mr. and Mrs. Ralph Bryan arrived here in 1926, bought a home and citrus grove, and raised two daughters, Barbara and Genevieve. This pioneer home included an orange grove and a citrus packing barn where fruit was shipped north. The property remained in the family until the father's death in 1976. (Courtesy of Port Orange Historical Trust.)

JACOB NAJARIAN'S HOME, 305 WELLMAN STREET, PORT ORANGE. Najarian was a barber for many years and owned a shop on Ridgewood Avenue, north of Dunlawton. This historic home was built in 1889 by George Boatright. Mrs. Aghaoni Najarian died in 1973, and Jacob died in 1985. (Courtesy of Port Orange Historical Trust.)

C.H. Meeker House, c. 1922, 4190 Halifax Drive. This is a rear view of the house, facing west. (Courtesy of Port Orange Historical Trust.)

Meeker House, Facing East, 4190 Halifax Drive. The house was originally built in 1887. Dr. Charles Meeker was an early settler of Port Orange and was instrumental in establishing the Grace Episcopal Church. Prior to building the sanctuary, church services were held in his home. Although this two-story home is judged to be frame vernacular, it has a gabled roof and chimney that provide interesting architectural lines. (Courtesy of Port Orange Historical Trust.)

WOODLAND CEMETERY, PORT ORANGE, FLORIDA. The grave sites of early settlers found here date back to the 1880s. (Courtesy of Port Orange Historical Trust.)

DR. H.K. DUBOIS, A PIONEER PHYSICIAN IN VOLUSIA COUNTY. DuBois was often seen around town as he traveled the area in his horse and buggy. He was often paid in eggs and produce for his home visits. (Courtesy of Port Orange Historical Trust.)

Dr. H.K. DuBois, First Mayor of Port Orange, 1913. Other town officers included A.M. Martin, clerk and assessor; A.J. Vass, marshall; J.M. Heath, collector; and S.C. Milburn, treasurer. (Courtesy of Port Orange Historical Trust.)

Four

TRANSPORTATION AND EARLY INDUSTRY

"BIG TREE," NEAR PORT ORANGE, FLORIDA. This tree was located on the south side of Big Tree Road and east of Nova Road. It met its demise in the early 1930s when a storm uprooted it. From the platform many local politicians inspired their constituents while they stood and mingled around this magnificent tree. It was a meeting place for many activities, including outdoor square dancing (with a "caller" atop the platform) during the days before the "horseless carriage" came into prominence. (Courtesy of Halifax Historical Society.)

A VIEW OF THE HALIFAX RIVER. This photo was taken from the porch of Riverside Inn in the early 1900s. (Courtesy of Port Orange Historical Trust.)

HENRY FLAGLER. Flagler was a pioneer who developed the Florida East Coast Railroad and many hotels and was thus known as the founder of the tourist industry on the east coast of Florida. (Courtesy of Halifax Historical Society.)

A "Grant" Locomotive with Two Pullman Cars, 1893. This engine had been rebuilt in 1875–1876. This historic locomotive and cars stopped at Port Orange during the 1890s when the depot first offered accommodations for passengers. (Courtesy of Florida East Coast Railroad.)

Port Orange Train Depot, 1910. The depot was built by Henry Flagler's Florida East Coast Railroad in 1894. Some of the prominent men of Port Orange posed for a special picture-taking event. This depot is one of the few original buildings still standing today. Notice the signs indicating segregated facilities. Passenger service was relinquished before World War II; however, freight service continued until around the 1950s. (Courtesy of Port Orange Historical Trust.)

PORT ORANGE TRAIN DEPOT. The depot was relocated to this site when Dunlawton was widened. Since relocation, it has been used as a roofing and pump warehouse. Today, it stands vacant. This depot was built when Henry Flagler was alive and is a valuable asset for Port Orange. The city plans to preserve it. The present location is north of Herbert Street at the railroad. (Courtesy of Port Orange Historical Trust.)

THE HAT FACTORY ON DUNLAWTON AVENUE, LATE 1890S. Hats were made from palmetto fronds that were cured and woven by the skilled hands of workers. This technique was an art form inherited by Floridians from the early Seminoles. These palmetto-style hats were very fashionable during this period and were especially popular with tourists. (Courtesy of Port Orange Historical Trust.)

AN UNIDENTIFIED FAMILY VISITING THE DUNLAWTON SUGAR MILL, C. 1899–1901. (Courtesy of Port Orange Historical Trust.)

DUNLAWTON AVENUE, LATE 1890S. The street was unpaved, and a horse and buggy sits in front of each of the two general stores. Pictured (bottom front) in the white shirt and black hat is local physician Dr. H.K. DuBois. Walking up the opposite side of the street (right center) is his wife, Florence. (Courtesy of Port Orange Historical Trust.)

DUNLAWTON AVENUE, LATE 1890S. This scene shows a horse and buggy beside a picket fence along a packed dirt road. This road ran west to the first town hall, school, and railroad. (Courtesy of Port Orange Historical Trust.)

ANNIE SIMCO'S HOME, BUILT C. 1888 The home, pictured in 1990, was used, at that time, as a minister's home for the Port Orange Baptist Church. It was originally located just south of the corner of U.S. 1 and Dunlawton Avenue. It was moved to a second site when U.S. 1 was widened to four lanes, and it served as a parsonage and church school until 1994 when it was demolished. Mrs. Simco was a descendant of the Fozzard family of early pioneers. She died several years prior to the relocation of the building. (Courtesy of Port Orange Historical Trust.)

PIONEER NEED–SMITH HOME ON HERBERT STREET, C. 1900. In later years the son, John Smith, raised his family here; however, time has taken its toll on this Florida Cracker–style home. (Courtesy of Port Orange Historical Trust.)

GRACE EPISCOPAL CHURCH, BUILT IN 1893, AND GUILD HALL, BUILT IN 1897. Grace Episcopal was one of the early churches and community centers in Port Orange. Dr. Charles Meeker, founder, came to the area in early 1875. Before the church was built, services were held in his home. Today, this church is one of our most outstanding buildings. The architectural style is Gothic Revival, and it has a steep-pitched, gabled roof with a bell tower. In the beginning, Guild Hall had several names, including Ridgewood Hall and Parrish Hall. (Courtesy of Port Orange Historical Trust.)

FARM CANE CRUSHER, 1905. Cane juice was boiled and cooled to sorghum syrup. It was then strained, poured into gallon jugs, and sold for home use. This animal-drawn machinery is located on the grounds of the Sugar Mill Botanical Gardens. (Courtesy of Cardwell Family Collection.)

SPRUCE CREEK CEMETERY. Many pioneer families are buried near the creek. Established before the turn of the century, the pioneer settlement and church that once stood nearby are now gone. Today, the fashionable Spruce Creek Fly-In subdivision, with private airport, encompasses this landmark. (Courtesy of Port Orange Historical Trust.)

AUSTIN T. SMITH'S FORMER HOME, BUILT C. 1890. The home was located at 3814 Halifax Drive at the river. A.T. Smith was a grocery store owner in Port Orange for many years. He also served as a toll collector on the second Port Orange Bridge. (Courtesy of Port Orange Historical Trust.)

EARLY SETTLER OTIS JOHNSON'S HOME ON LOUISVILLE STREET, PORT ORANGE, C. 1905. A landmark that stood for many years, this house was demolished in 1998. (Courtesy of Port Orange Historical Trust.)

Dr. H.K. DuBois's Home on Halifax Drive in Port Orange. This house partially burned in the early 1950s. Later, it was used as a restaurant, and finally, it became a funeral home. It still stands today. (Courtesy of Port Orange Historical Trust.)

Lyon and Stover's Lumber Company Delivery Wagon, before World War I. The lumber yard was located on the west side of the railroad at Herbert Street. In the early days, lumber was delivered to the building site by horse and wagon until trucks came into use after World War I. The lumber company could furnish all building supplies that were needed to complete a home or store. This company ceased operation prior to World War II. (Courtesy of Port Orange Historical Trust.)

Dr. H.K. DuBois. Dr. DuBois is pictured in the yard of his fashionable home at 4084 Halifax Drive. (Courtesy of Port Orange Historical Trust.)

An Early Photo of the First Port Orange Bridge, Built 1906. This toll bridge was 1 mile long, cost $22,000 to build, and was designed by Sumner Hale Gove. George Lufberry, a principal in the Port Orange Bridge Company, deeded 120 acres toward the development of the east side of the Port Orange Bridge project. (Courtesy of Port Orange Historical Trust.)

THE WEST END OF THE OLD WOODEN PORT ORANGE BRIDGE IN THE 1920S. It met its demise during a storm in 1932. (Courtesy of Port Orange Historical Trust.)

PORT ORANGE HOUSE. Since 1872, this old landmark has undergone several name changes, including Grandview Sanitarium, Alligator Inn, and Riverview Apartments. This structure was deemed uninhabitable and was demolished, *c.* 1997. (Courtesy of Port Orange Historical Trust.)

PORT ORANGE DRAWBRIDGE AND TOLL HOUSE, C. 1927. The toll house was the residence of the bridge tenders, of whom there were several over the years. Among the last were the Holbert sisters, who kept chickens on a small island under the bridge. During high tide or a storm, the flock had to be rescued. (Courtesy of Port Orange Historical Trust.)

OLD WOODEN PORT ORANGE BRIDGE, LATE 1920S. On Sunday afternoons, visitors often drove along the shore of the scenic Halifax River, occasionally stopping to view the beautiful subtropical landscape. (Courtesy of Port Orange Historical Trust.)

PORT ORANGE BRIDGE, 1910. Oscar Mann held the position as bridge tender for many years. In later years, the wheels of a truck fell through the planking, and it took several days to remove the obstacle. (Courtesy of Port Orange Historical Trust.)

THE AFRICAN-AMERICAN SCHOOL, C. 1920S, ON NORTH ORANGE AVENUE AND MAGNOLIA STREET. The first school was on Dunlawton Avenue; however, when the railroad came through, it was relocated to the North Orange Avenue site. Some of the children who attended this school were descendants of the failed colony of Dr. John Milton Hawks. The outdated books from the white school were passed down to the African-American school. (Courtesy of Port Orange Historical Trust.)

Five
CULTURAL CHANGES

FIRST UNITED METHODIST CHURCH OF PORT ORANGE, 1906. This sanctuary was demolished in 1962 to make way for the structure that stands today. The church was organized in 1895. (Courtesy of Port Orange Historical Trust.)

MT. MORIAH BAPTIST CHURCH, C. 1910. This church was dedicated in 1911 and serves the African-American people of Freemanville, a community near the railroad, west of U.S. 1. Over the years, the population of the settlement has changed many times. The last time the church was renovated was 1956. The facade has remained virtually unchanged, although minor repairs have been made throughout the years. (Courtesy of Port Orange Historical Trust.)

JOHN TEDDER HOME, 1910. The Tedders were a pioneer family of Port Orange; their descendants still live in the area. (Courtesy of Port Orange Historical Trust.)

JACK OSTEEN'S FORMER HOME, BUILT C. 1910. Osteen was the former mayor of Port Orange. This house is located at 3786 Halifax Drive on the river. (Courtesy of Port Orange Historical Trust.)

TOWNSLEY HOME, 1914. Frank Townsley played a significant role in the development of Port Orange. This bungalow-style home is located at 4316 Halifax Drive. (Courtesy of Port Orange Historical Trust.)

DR. J.M. MASTERS'S SANITARIUM. Masters operated this sanitarium as a part of the Old Alligator Inn at the northwest corner of Halifax Drive and Dunlawton Avenue. The convalescents stayed at this facility during the years 1912 to 1924, between the months of November and May. Each year they arrived at the Port Orange Depot by Pullman car and made their way to the sanitarium by hack or jitney service. Many patients suffered from consumption and other lung ailments. (Courtesy of Cardwell Family Collection, 1976.)

THE TRIBBLE INN, C. 1912, ON DUNLAWTON AVENUE AND U.S. 1. Rooms were available by the night, the week, or the month. In later years, it was called the Port Orange Inn. Some of the local school teachers took up residence at the inn; however, the owners depended primarily on the tourist trade. Square dances were often held in the dining room. (Courtesy of Port Orange Historical Trust.)

FIRST PORT ORANGE SCHOOL ON THE SOUTHWEST CORNER OF DUNLAWTON AND ORANGE AVENUES, C. 1916. The middle section of the building pictured was constructed in 1889. Later, after the turn of the century, two other sections were added. When the new brick building was constructed in 1925, the old wooden structure became a multi-purpose building. The old building was moved three times before its demise in the late 1960s. (Courtesy of Port Orange Historical Trust.)

DUNLAWTON HISTORIC DISTRICT, DUNLAWTON AVENUE, C. 1901. The white house, pictured in the foreground, was the home of Thelma Houghton, a Port Orange school teacher and postmistress. (Courtesy of Cardwell Family Collection.)

HISTORIC DISTRICT, DUNLAWTON AVENUE. This photo was taken in 1999. (Courtesy of Cardwell Family Collection.)

HOMES IN THE NATIONAL HISTORIC DISTRICT. This view is looking west on Dunlawton, between Lafayette and Orange Avenues. (Courtesy of Port Orange Historical Trust.)

DUNLAWTON PLANTATION, C. 1900. Three local visitors pose on a mule-drawn buckboard positioned between the sugar mill house and the boiler room. This mill, partially destroyed during the Second Seminole Indian War (1835–1842), was rebuilt by John Marshall, a planter, in 1849. (Courtesy of Port Orange Historical Trust.)

THE WEDDING CHAPEL. This chapel is located on the grounds of the Sugar Mill Botanical Gardens. Visitors have come to these gardens for family outings through the years. Today, the site is a popular outdoor wedding chapel. (Courtesy of Port Orange Historical Trust.)

EARLY CITRUS INDUSTRY. After the Civil War, the citrus industry boomed on the east coast of Florida. In 1894, 1895, and 1899, disastrous freezes almost wiped out the industry. However, it regained its prominence after the turn of the century. Later, after World War II, freezes again caused the citrus growers to relocate and plant their groves further south. Over the years, Port Orange was affected by the relocation of citrus growers and, today, subdivisions stand where pioneer orange groves were once planted. (Courtesy of Halifax Historical Society.)

DOROTHY PRICE AND FRIENDS, IN FRONT OF HER HOME ON RIVERSIDE DRIVE IN PORT ORANGE, 1915. Pictured from left to right are Mary Carrow, Hazel McDonald, Callie Yelvington, and Dorothy Price. These young ladies were the daughters of early settlers who helped build Port Orange. (Courtesy of Port Orange Historical Trust.)

"Old Joe," a Favorite Attraction of Tourists and Locals Alike. The alligator was maintained in a fenced pond at the rear of Riverview Apartments. After many years, Old Joe became a nuisance for local residents because of his loud bellowing sounds at night. He was finally moved to an alligator farm near U.S. 1 and Big Tree Road. Jim Patillo (pictured) said that Old Joe was probably around 100 years old. However, the age of Old Joe was apparently exaggerated. Research has revealed that alligators live in captivity into their mid-70s. Old Joe's absence from the pond simply made way for frogs making complaining sounds at night. Eventually, the pond was eliminated and finally there were quiet nights in the neighborhood. (Courtesy of Port Orange Historical Trust.)

GAMBLE HOUSE ("EGWANULTI," NATIVE AMERICAN FOR "BY THE WATER"), SOUTH SIDE VIEW, 1986. James N. Gamble, while on a hunting expedition up Spruce Creek in 1897, bought the house from a settler for use as a hunting camp. In later years, he built the cracker-style building, planted an orange grove, and constructed a small citrus packing barn. Following Gamble's death in 1938, his son-in-law, Judge Alfred Nippert, built a replica of the Snow White house and mine shaft nearby for his young daughter, who was enchanted by the famous movie and story *Snow White and the Seven Dwarfs*. Gamble was owner of the Proctor and Gamble Company. Today this property is utilized, and owned, by Nature's Conservancy. The caretakers are the Museum of Arts and Sciences and the City of Port Orange. (Courtesy of Port Orange Historical Trust.)

GAMBLE HOUSE ("EGWANULTI"), 1986. Pictured is a front view of the south side facing Spruce Creek. James Gamble often brought his yacht up the shallows of Spruce Creek to the dockside of the retreat. This preserve has very old cypress trees, live oaks, and long leaf yellow pines. Also, there is a very old magnolia tree and a wild olive tree, making the property a valuable asset for nature lovers. (Courtesy of Port Orange Historical Trust.)

GAMBLE PLACE DOCK AT SPRUCE CREEK, C. 1939. James Gamble piloted his yacht up Spruce Creek to his dock. Notice the Sabal palms leaning out over the water, which produces a tropical effect. (Courtesy of Port Orange Historical Trust.)

FRED STONE (LEFT) AND JIM JACKSON (RIGHT). The man on the horse-drawn wagon is unidentified. (Courtesy of Port Orange Historical Trust.)

A LOCAL HUNTING PARTY NEAR PORT ORANGE, FLORIDA, C. 1920. Pictured from left to right are Jim Jackson, Rolly Johnson, Louis Dees, and Fred Stone. (Courtesy of Port Orange Historical Trust.)

PORT ORANGE JITNEY SERVICE, C. 1925. The vehicle seen here, on Dunlawton Avenue, was used to transport passengers to the train depot and inns, and for beach and countryside tours. During inclement weather, drop-curtains were utilized. (Courtesy of Halifax Historical Society.)

Six
WORLD WAR I AND THE LAND BOOM

DUNLAWTON AVENUE, PORT ORANGE, C. 1920. This scene shows the Guam Apartments on the right. Notice the sidewalks and electric light pole. The roadbeds consisted of local white marl as a base, with a shell top as a covering. (Courtesy of Port Orange Historical Trust.)

JAMES N. GAMBLE (SECOND FROM LEFT) AT JOE WILLIAMS' HOUSE NEAR LEVINE LANDING AT SPRUCE CREEK. Pictured with him, from left to right, are Jim Jackson, Mr. Gamble, Dr. Gorbisouce, Rolly Jackson, Sally Jackson, Elsie Johnson, Morley Bugher, Helen Eger, Fred Johnson's two children (names unknown), Fred Johnson, and Dr. Gengler. (Courtesy of Port Orange Historical Trust.)

BATHING SUITS OF 1921. Marion Stover (left) was the daughter of a local lumber dealer, and Dorothy Price (right) was the daughter of a local building contractor. The 1921 bathing suits were made of wool, and a bathing cap was usually worn. Most people from Port Orange walked to the beach, crossing the old wooden bridge, to avoid paying the toll. (Courtesy of Port Orange Historical Trust.)

WILLIAM E. SANDS HOUSE, BUILT 1923. This frame vernacular house is located at 3512 Halifax Drive. Sands owned the Oyster House Market located across from his home. For many years his name was synonymous with fresh oysters from the Halifax River. The quality of their seafood was known far and wide. (Courtesy of Port Orange Historical Trust.)

FLORIDA EAST COAST RAILROAD—ENGINE NO. 802, WITH FREIGHT CARS. This historic locomotive passed through Port Orange for many years with freight, and during the winter season, laden with citrus for the northern market. In 1925, an additional track was constructed to accommodate both north- and south-bound trains. (Courtesy of Florida East Coast Railroad.)

PORT ORANGE LIBRARY AND LITERARY CLUB. The library was located at the northeast corner of Herbert Street and Ridgewood Avenue in the early 1920s. This was the first library in Port Orange. (Courtesy of Port Orange Historical Trust.)

```
            GREETINGS
              from
         PORT ORANGE, FLORIDA.

   The Literary and Library Club
   Is building a new home;
   All members plan to work like ants,
   (No matter where they roam)
   In making lots of pretty things,
   In asking for them too,
   And this explains the postal card
   We hope may interest you.

   We aim to have a grand bazaar,
   Thus helping pay our debt.
   We have our lot, with cash in bank;
   Yet many things to get.
   We're promised a complete house
   The first day of November.
   This fete to be our house-warming
   The ninth day or December

   We hope to have a goodley show
   Of articles to sell
   For Christmas gifts to send away,
   And for home-folks as well.

   We need things for our different booths.
   No gift will be amiss;
   Please send us what you'd like to buy,
   In a bazaar like this,
   And every member of the club
   Will glory in your gift,
   And be enthused to forge ahead
   With every helpful lift.
          Yours for success
       Miss Alice M. Wakeley, Pres.
       Mrs. E. D. Chapman, Vice Pres.
       Mrs. Kate Jordan Hewett,
                Chairman Committee
       Mrs. Bush Niel Garnsey,
                Vice-Chairman Committee
```

POSTCARD GREETINGS. This was a promotional card sent to solicit funds for the first library in Port Orange. (Courtesy of Port Orange Historical Trust.)

EARLY SPRUCE CREEK SCHOOL, C. 1920S. Among the mostly unidentified students pictured is the late Hazel Fenty (front row, second from right), past president of the Port Orange Historical Trust. In the village area, there was once a sawmill, a church, and two cemeteries. This school structure was located near the north bank of Spruce Creek at the entrance to the fly-in airport, and the golf course off Taylor Road today. (Courtesy of Port Orange Historical Trust.)

PORT ORANGE SCHOOL, EIGHTH GRADE CLASS, 1920. Pictured from left to right are the following: (front row) Ida Sparkman and Naaman Apple (a winter visitor); (middle row) Crawford Earnhart, Marshall Patillo, Cora Morford, Fred Nicholson, Lois Carron, and Mable Sparkman; (back row) Reba Stone, Mrs. Eugenia Fair (teacher), and Gustaf Rast. (Courtesy of Port Orange Historical Trust.)

PORT ORANGE SCHOOL FACULTY, 1925. Pictured from left to right are C. Lindsey (principal), Nannie Hines, Sylvia Kerfoot, Lottie Wells, Mrs. Thelma Houghton, Laura Tyler, Sylas Franklin, and Edward Haller. (Courtesy of Port Orange Historical Trust.)

PORT ORANGE SCHOOL FACULTY, MAY 1926. Pictured from left to right are the following: (front row) Mr. Dewey Wells, Mr. Sylas Franklin, and Mr. B.E. Jones; (back row) Miss Sylvia Kerfoot, Mrs. Thelma Houghton, Miss Lucille Swadner, Miss Cora Morford, Mrs. Mary Spicer, Miss Laura Tyler, and Miss Nannie Hines. (Courtesy of Port Orange Historical Trust.)

FLORENCE BRACEY DUBOIS, BEHIND THE WHEEL OF A 1925 FORD MODEL T COUPE. She was the wife of Dr. H.K. DuBois, who practiced medicine in Port Orange, Florida. (Courtesy of Florida State Archives.)

PORT ORANGE SCHOOL, APRIL 1927. The school was built in 1925 at a cost of $31,890 by architect William J. Carpenter of St. Petersburg, Florida, and builder Donald F. Douglass, a native of New Smyrna Beach, Florida. An eight-room addition was added to the original building in 1941, and it was enlarged again in 1954. Modernization has occurred to the present day. Today, this is one of the elementary schools in Port Orange. (Courtesy of Port Orange Historical Trust.)

MRS. THELMA HOUGHTON, RETIRED SCHOOL TEACHER AND FORMER POSTMISTRESS. Mrs. Houghton was very active in the Port Orange Historical Trust until her death in 1993. She taught in the Port Orange School on the corner of Orange and Dunlawton Avenues for many years, and worked at the post office on East Dunlawton. (Courtesy of Port Orange Historical Trust.)

C.F. FEDOR, FISHING FROM THE PORT ORANGE BRIDGE IN THE SUMMER OF 1925. This structure was a popular fishing place and was utilized as a pier even after it could no longer be used as a bridge. (Courtesy of Port Orange Historical Trust.)

GANYMEDE ARCH, 1925, SOUTH DAYTONA, FLORIDA. Ridge Road is the street going into the subdivision today. During the real estate "boom," this subdivision had grandiose plans. The arch was completed, along with seven model homes. All the main streets were laid out, the sidewalks were put in, but the streets were never paved. The architecture of the homes was Mediterranean Revival with a red barrel tile roof. A large hotel and golf course were planned, but never constructed. Today the old Spanish-style model homes are still standing amid a beautiful community of modern residences. Unfortunately, this magnificent arch was demolished in the 1950s to accommodate the widening of U.S. 1. (Courtesy of Port Orange Historical Trust.)

JIM BENNETT'S HOME ON HERBERT STREET, PORT ORANGE. This home is located west of present-day Nova Road, and is one of the "boom time" stucco homes which is of a vernacular architecture. Jim Bennett was the son of a pioneer family whose descendants are still living in Port Orange today. (Courtesy of Port Orange Historical Trust.)

A.T. SMITH AND COLONEL TEDDER. Smith and Tedder (behind the counter from left to right) are pictured in their early grocery store and meat market on Ridgewood Avenue with three unidentified customers, c. 1927. (Courtesy of Port Orange Historical Trust.)

OSBORNE HALL IN 1986, SOUTHSIDE OF DUNLAWTON AVENUE BETWEEN U.S. 1 AND LAFAYETTE. Osborne Hall was a multi-purpose fraternity hall, and in 1929 it was the state headquarters for the Ku Klux Klan. It is alleged that they practiced their rituals on Dunlawton Avenue at night. Over the years it was used as a youth recreation hall, a small boat building facility (downstairs), as a feed and seed store, and as a candle factory. Sponsors boasted that the upstairs had the finest dance floor around, made of tongue-in-groove pine. (Courtesy of Port Orange Historical Trust.)

WILBUR HOTEL AT WILBUR-BY-THE-SEA, 1930. The hotel was constructed from local Coquina stone, which was brought by flat-boat from a quarry at Spruce Creek. (Courtesy of Port Orange Historical Trust.)

ECKERSEN'S GARAGE, 1930. This was a well-known family, and Nat Eckersen was a skilled auto mechanic. Nat once stated that during prohibition a "gangster type" appeared at his home late one night demanding that his car be repaired. The well-dressed individual indicated that he had a gun, and Nat obliged his request. After the repair was completed, the "rum-runner" showed his gratitude by paying Nat a substantial amount of money and then drove off into the night. (Courtesy of Port Orange Historical Trust.)

PORT ORANGE HOTEL, C. 1930, A.T. SMITH, PROPRIETOR. Notice the sign indicating the room rates and services offered. (Courtesy of Port Orange Historical Trust.)

DAVE'S DOCK AT THE FOOT OF PORT ORANGE BRIDGE, C. 1938. For many years this was a favorite for fisherman; a boat could be rented and the best live bait could be purchased. Fishing tackle and river information was always readily available. After the second Port Orange Bridge was built, following World War II, a restaurant was constructed dockside which was known as Dave's Dock Restaurant for many years. Today it is Aunt Catfish's and is known for its seafood. (Courtesy of Port Orange Historical Trust.)

RIVERSIDE DRIVE, ALLANDALE, FLORIDA. Travelers saw this scenic view, along what was Old Dixie Highway, many years ago on their journey to West Palm Beach and Miami. (Courtesy of Port Orange Historical Trust.)

CITY HALL/ PUBLIC LIBRARY, WITH OLD SPANISH KETTLE IN FRONT, ALLANDALE, FLORIDA. This is an obsolete syrup kettle (right, foreground) from the plantation period, origin unknown. There were 16 plantations from New Smyrna to Pellicer Creek, all involved in sugar making during the Second Spanish and Territorial Periods in Florida. This kettle was an identity symbol for Allandale. (Courtesy of Port Orange Historical Trust.)

SITE OF THE FORMER DIXIE HIGHWAY BRIDGE CROSSING ROSE BAY, C. 1913. Old Dixie Highway was the first paved road leading southward to Miami. (Courtesy of Cardwell Family Collection.)

Seven
THE GREAT DEPRESSION

DOWNTOWN PORT ORANGE, C. 1930S. Pictured are Port Orange Hotel and A.T. Smith's Grocery Store. Smith's is now Count's Western Wear, still located on the northeast corner of U.S. 1 and Dunlawton Avenue. Seen across the street from left to right are Waldron's Sundries, Port Orange State Bank, Tedder's Meat Market, A&P Grocery Store, a cafe, and a tavern. In the late 1960s, the southside building was demolished to accommodate the widening of U.S. 1. The Port Orange State Bank closed in 1932. (Courtesy of Port Orange Historical Trust.)

COLONEL TEDDER'S MEAT MARKET, MID-1930S. The market was located south of Dunlawton Avenue on Ridgewood Avenue. Colonel Tedder was a butcher for many years and his store was noted for its high-quality meats and excellent service. Pictured to the right is Dan Doty, helper. (Courtesy of Port Orange Historical Trust.)

HAROLD "DOC" AND MINNIE WALDRON'S HOME, CORNER OF DUNLAWTON AND U.S. 1. The home was a landmark for many years, and it is alleged that the previous owner had a secret crawl-space under the floor where he stored illicit liquor for resale. Doc Waldron operated Waldron's Sundries on the east side of U.S. 1. (Courtesy of Port Orange Historical Trust.)

TYPICAL FLORIDA "CRACKER"-STYLE HOME NEAR PORT ORANGE, LATE 1920S. This structure features an open porch, raised wood floor, double hung windows for cross ventilation, and a pitched shingle roof. (Courtesy of Port Orange Historical Trust.)

MOODY BRIDGE, C. 1932. This bridge, named for a local pioneer land owner, is located west of Port Orange, connecting Airport Road with Spruce Creek. The bridge was raised in the middle to allow James N. Gamble's yacht to reach his dock, located up Spruce Creek. (Courtesy of Port Orange Historical Trust.)

JOE MILLER'S LITTLE CAR, WITH HIS SON, ROY, SEATED. Standing from left to right are the Shipes brothers: Charley, Marvin, Joseph and Irwin—all local residents of Port Orange in the 1930s. Roy Miller later became a college English professor. (Courtesy of Port Orange Historical Trust.)

CITY OF PORT ORANGE BASEBALL CLUB, C. 1932. Pictured from left to right are the following: (top row) Delbert Brooks, L.T. Sansbury, Sam Lemon, Jesse Yelvington, Fred Donaldville, David Eckerson, and Dennis Sykes; (kneeling) W.D. Foust, "Doc" Waldron, Ed Carlton, unidentified, and Stanley Houghton. (Courtesy of Port Orange Historical Trust.)

MAY POLE DANCE, IN FRONT OF THE OLD WOODEN PORT ORANGE SCHOOL, C. 1930. This colorful dance was part of the annual school program for girls and boys. (Courtesy of Port Orange Historical Trust.)

SIR MALCOLM CAMPBELL AND HIS "BLUEBIRD" RACER ON THE BEACH. He was here for speed trials in 1928 (206.95 mph), 1931 (245.73 mph), 1932 (253.96 mph), 1933 (272.108 mph), and 1935 (276.816 mph). He was knighted by the English crown for his land speed records. The south end of the measured mile was at the Dunlawton approach, across the river from Port Orange—today it is Daytona Beach Shores. (Courtesy of John Gontner.)

MAJOR HENRY O'NEILL DEHANE SEGRAVE, 1929. Segrave is making a trial run on the beach across the bridge from Port Orange—the measured mile. The measured mile calculates the speed of the racer through marked mile posts, which read from instruments atop a timing tower. The racer must build up speed several miles before entering the measured mile area. This was done by making the run going north, and then south, to obtain the average calculated speed. (Courtesy of Port Orange Historical Trust.)

MEASURED MILE BEACH TOWER, 1932. This structure served many of the ground-speed record trials through the measured mile. The more famous drivers, who set records, were Lockhart, Segrave, and Campbell. It ceased as an instrument tower in 1935. The average speed was set by running the measured mile south and running the measured mile north. (Courtesy of Port Orange Historical Trust.)

BEACH RACES—SOUTH TURN, AT DEMOTTE STREET, 1940. Notice the Ford Coup, a popular race car, rounding the south turn. The north turn was where Daytona Beach Shores City Hall is located today. The first road/beach course was 3.5 miles. (Courtesy of John Gontner.)

REENACTMENT OF THE MEASURED MILE SPEED TRIALS—CLASSIC CAR EVENT, FEBRUARY 14, 1995. (Courtesy of Cardwell Family Collection.)

L.T. Sansbury (left), Principal of Port Orange School, with Teachers Mitchell Shemear (center) and Clyde Flowers (right). Mr. Shemear taught physical education and civics, and Mr. Flowers taught science during the junior high school years. Students had to ride the bus to Mainland High School to complete their senior years (11th and 12th grades). (Courtesy of Port Orange Historical Trust.)

Port Orange Softball Team, late 1930s. L.T. Sansbury (left, standing) and Mitchell Shemear (right, standing) are pictured with unidentified members of the team. Softball was a popular sport during the Depression; other teams in competition were Holly Hill and Ormond. (Courtesy of Port Orange Historical Trust.)

JUDGE THOMAS J. SPARKMAN HOME, A 1931 FRAME VERNACULAR STRUCTURE, AT 810 ORANGE AVENUE. Sparkman was an early pioneer and elected as representative to the Florida Legislature, 1901–1905. Later he served as justice of the peace for the Port Orange area. (Courtesy of Port Orange Historical Trust.)

THE ORIGINAL SITE OF JAKE NAJARIAN'S BARBER SHOP, 3977 SOUTH RIDGEWOOD AVENUE. Today it is the home of Razor's Barber Shop. Jake was a barber for over half a century in Port Orange. Old-timers can remember sitting on a board, across the arms of the chair, for their early childhood haircuts. (Courtesy of Port Orange Historical Trust.)

FAITH CHAPEL PENTECOSTAL HOLINESS CHURCH IN 1950, 633 HERBERT STREET. This building replaced the old pioneer church (built 1937) that now houses the fellowship hall. (Courtesy of Port Orange Historical Trust.)

FAITH CHAPEL, FELLOWSHIP HALL, 1937, 633 HERBERT STREET. The church's first founder and minister was Mrs. M. "Sister Mack" McDonald. This was a pioneer church and Mrs. McDonald was well respected in the community. For many years she also drove the Port Orange School bus. (Courtesy of Port Orange Historical Trust.)

DAVE'S DOCK, 1939. Phil Culpepper (left) and Russell Smith (right) are pictured in front of Dave's Dock, located on the south side of the old Port Orange Bridge, Today this is the site of Aunt Catfish's Restaurant. Dave's Dock was a popular place to rent a boat and fishing tackle, buy bait, and obtain information for fishing on the Halifax River. (Courtesy of Port Orange Historical Trust.)

PORT ORANGE SCHOOL, SIXTH GRADE CLASS, MAY DAY PROGRAM, 1939. "The King of May" was Merle Carter, and "The Queen of May" was Julia Grace Swain. The identified student followers (not listed in order) were George Patterson, Mary Margaret Frederick, Harley Merry, Charlie Merry, Charlotte Lester, Francis Robinson, and one unidentified young boy. (Courtesy of Port Orange Historical Trust.)

FIRST BAPTIST CHURCH ON CHURCH STREET, C. 1939. Pictured is a large group of unidentified Sunday worshippers. Established in 1924, the old sanctuary was built in 1931. Because of the growth of the population of Port Orange in more recent years, the church has divided into several other congregations. A new sanctuary was built in 1961, on the same site. (Courtesy of Port Orange Historical Trust.)

PORT ORANGE CIVIL LEADERS. Pictured from left to right are Roy Clifton, local law enforcement officer; George Patterson, who eventually became city clerk; Shorty Shipes, a city service station owner; and Wilbur Willis, who eventually became mayor. They oversaw the clearing of city property and the right-of-way. (Courtesy of Port Orange Historical Trust.)

PORT ORANGE LAW ENFORCEMENT OF THE 1930S, 1940S, AND 1950S. Seen from left to right are Russ Galbreath, Theo Nicholson, and Roy Clifton. (Courtesy of Port Orange Historical Trust.)

FLORIDA EAST COAST RAILWAY. Engine No. 446 passed through Port Orange each day, dropping off and picking up mail on its routes north and south. It is shown here with mail and pullman cars. (Florida East Coast Railroad.)

AERIAL VIEW OF PORT ORANGE, FLORIDA, 1939. The 1906 bridge over the Halifax River collapsed and met its demise in 1932. U.S. 1 and Dunlawton Avenue were two-lane roads, as four-lane roads did not exist until after World War II. (Courtesy of Port Orange Historical Trust.)

Eight
WORLD WAR II AND POST WAR

AERIAL VIEW OF SEA BIRD ISLAND MOBILE HOME PARK, HALIFAX RIVER, C. 1980. The second Port Orange Bridge, built in 1951, was eventually torn down to make way for the present "high-span" bridge in 1990. (Courtesy of Cardwell Family Collection.)

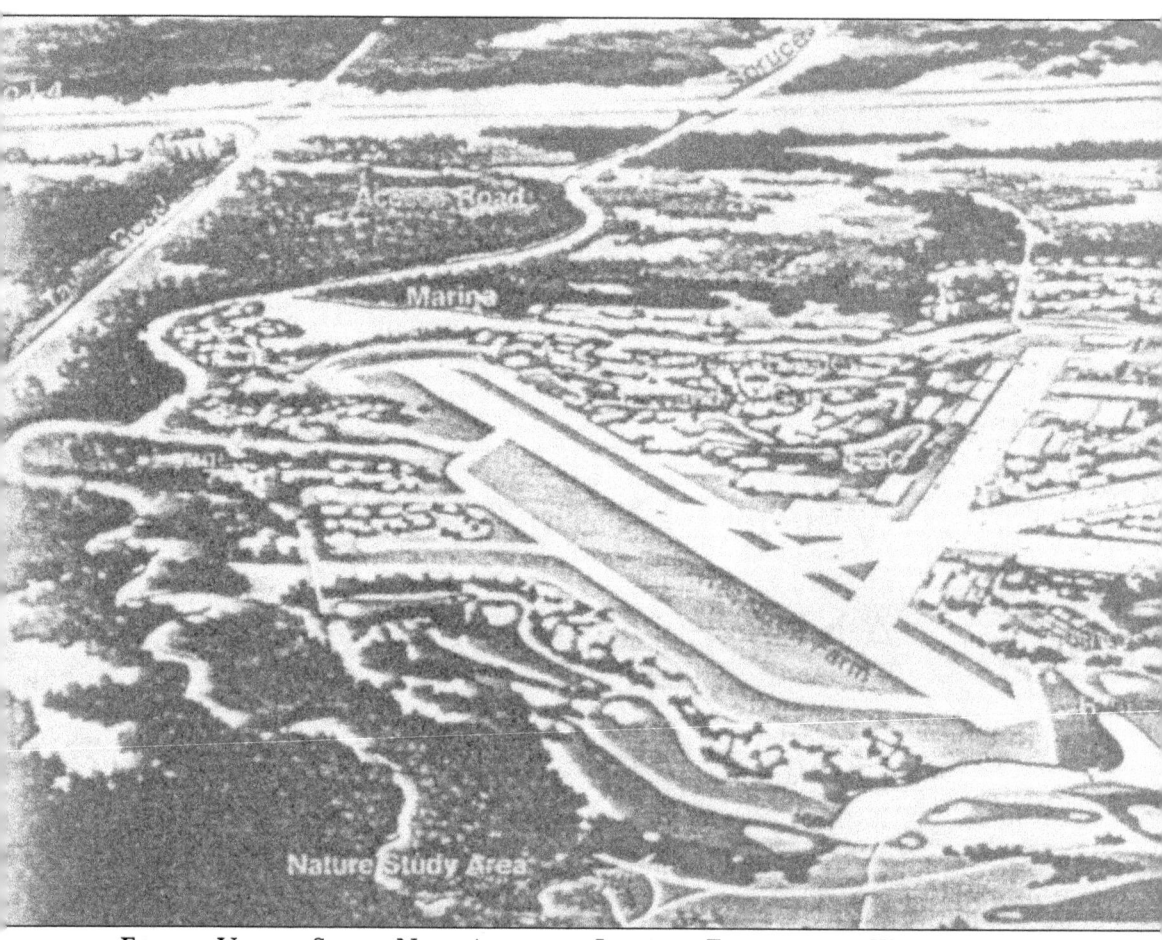

FORMER UNITED STATES NAVY AUXILIARY LANDING FIELD DURING WORLD WAR II, FROM 1942 TO 1946. Navy fliers practiced carrier landings on these runways. These pilots had already earned their wings and, upon completion of this training, they were sent to join the Navy fleet in the Pacific Theater of War. The picture above is an artist's later rendering of the proposed plan for the Spruce Creek Fly-In Airport Subdivision. (Courtesy of Port Orange Historical Trust.)

SPRUCE CREEK FLY-IN AIRPORT. During World War II, this was a United States Navy Auxiliary Landing Field. Navy pilots practiced carrier-landings on this runway. (Courtesy of Port Orange Historical Trust.)

THE CHAMPION, FLORIDA EAST COAST RAILROAD, ENGINE NO. 1003. For many years this streamliner locomotive passed through Port Orange on the north and south bound tracks. It was one of the most recognized and talked about trains because of its high standard of service in dining, pullman, and coaches. Today there is no passenger service passing through Port Orange, and only one track accommodates both north and south directions. (Courtesy of Port Orange Historical Trust.)

CLUB "400," RIDGEWOOD AVENUE, NORTH OF PORT ORANGE. The club was constructed in the early 1930s and was known as "Farmer Dan's" for many years. The early menu featured a half-chicken on toast for 25¢. During World War II it was a popular night club frequented by servicemen from nearby military bases. In later years, it was changed to "Bucky's Five O'Clock Club" and was eventually demolished in the early 1960s. (Courtesy of Port Orange Historical Trust.)

PORT ORANGE BUSLINE, C. 1940S. The bus driver was Charlie Shipes, a well-respected citizen, who went out of his way to accommodate the passengers. Charlie was always friendly and cheerful, and well liked. Occasionally, he would amuse riders with remarks or stories. The route ran from Port Orange to Daytona Beach, and returned several times daily on schedule. (Courtesy of Port Orange Historical Trust.)

PORT ORANGE SCHOOL BAND, 1942. Among the mostly unidentified band members are Gary Rumley (front row, third from left); Harold D. Cardwell Sr. (back row, sixth from left); and Saraphine Gardner (front row, far right, seated). (Courtesy of Port Orange Historical Trust.)

UNITED STATES ARMY AIR FORCE OBSERVER ARM-BAND, IDENTIFICATION CARDS, AND OFFICIAL HANDBOOK. Volunteers during World War II were issued this arm-band and accessories. The observation deck was constructed on a platform under the water tower. They recorded all planes that flew north and south along the Florida coast. The citizens performed a very important service for the war effort from 1942 to 1945. (Courtesy of Halifax Historical Society.)

L.T. SANSBURY, LIEUTENANT, U.S. NAVY. Sansbury was drafted at the beginning of World War II, which temporarily interrupted his teaching career. Following the war, he resumed his administrative duties as principal for the Port Orange School. Upon his retirement as principal, he became the mayor of the City of Port Orange. (Courtesy of Port Orange Historical Trust.)

PORT ORANGE SCHOOL GRADUATING CLASS OF 1942. Students pictured are as follows, from left to right: (front row) Floyd Metts, Mary Margaret Frederick, Alma McDonald, Elinor Baggett, and Homer Chance; (middle row) Bill Thompson, Harold D. Cardwell Sr., Roy Eckersen, Junior Poucher, Dougherty Smith, Howard Jones, George Patterson, and Raymond Rose; (back row, faculty) Mrs. O. Smith, Robert Chanter, Mrs. Ida Patterson, L.T. Sansbury (principal), and Mrs. Clyde Flowers. (Courtesy of Cardwell Family Collection.)

PORT ORANGE SCHOOL, 1943. Priscilla Rumley-Cardwell is holding the slate designating the fifth grade class. (Courtesy of Port Orange Historical Trust.)

ATLANTIC GARAGE AND FILLING STATION, ON THE NORTHWEST CORNER OF DUNLAWTON AVENUE AND U.S. 1. Mr. Bill Rutter operated this station for many years after World War II. A portion of the former city hall, with its open-air porch, can be seen in the background, on the left of the filling station. In the rear is the city water tower. (Courtesy of Port Orange Historical Trust.)

HOME OF ARLIE AND HETTIE CARDWELL, 770 HERBERT STREET, BUILT C. 1948. Long-time residents of Port Orange, Arlie died in 1982 and Hettie died in 1989. This photo was taken July 4, 1999. For many years, the Cardwell Plant Farm and Sugar Mill Landscape Nurseries were adjoined to this property. (Courtesy of Cardwell Family Collection.)

PORT ORANGE CITY HALL, 1947. This building served as city hall until a new, modern city complex was built in the 1990s. Eventually it was torn down to allow for the widening of Dunlawton and an entry to a shopping center. The population growth of Port Orange required moving the city center westward and providing larger facilities for the city government. (Courtesy of Port Orange Historical Trust.)

WILBUR WILLIS, MAYOR OF PORT ORANGE, 1949–1969. This outstanding mayor was a true politician who knew how to deal with the city council to get things done. He was well known in the community and dealt with the city's rapid growth. He was instrumental in the development of the police and fire departments, the city's water and sewage, the paving of streets, and city government operations. Willis was the first baby born in Wilbur-by-the-Sea, and he was given the name of his birthplace. (Courtesy of Port Orange Historical Trust.)

PORT ORANGE FIRE DEPARTMENT, DUNLAWTON AVENUE. This double-door structure was built after the end of World War II. The all-volunteer operation utilized two fire trucks—an old LaFrance and a new Ford pumper-truck. (Courtesy of Port Orange Historical Trust.)

EARLY PORT ORANGE FIRE TRUCKS IN FRONT OF THE FORMER CITY HALL BUILDING. The oldest truck (right) was a 1924 LaFrance, and the truck on the left was a 1947 Ford. This early equipment of the Port Orange Fire Department was operated by volunteers. (Courtesy of Port Orange Historical Trust.)

BUCK'S BARN, 1955. "The World's Best Bar-B-Que" was served in South Daytona by Buck Buchanan, who operated a gas station and bar-b-que for many years. Eventually this building was renovated and became a night club. Later, it was torn down and today it is the site of the new South Daytona City Hall. (Courtesy of Port Orange Historical Trust.)

GRACE EPISCOPAL CHURCH, 1893; AND GUILD HALL (FORMERLY RIDGEWOOD HALL), 1897, RIDGEWOOD AVENUE. This sanctuary and hall are outstanding landmarks of old Port Orange. (Courtesy of Port Orange Historical Trust.)

MOTORCYCLE RACING ON THE BEACH AT PONCE INLET, FEBRUARY 25, 1952. The second Port Orange Bridge was opened in 1951, which helped alleviate race traffic and provided easier access for emergency vehicles. (Courtesy of John Gontner.)

BEACH RACES—NORTH TURN, PONCE INLET, 1955. This is where the cars left the beach and made the north turn onto the pavement. As they made the turn, cars slid sideways and slung sand, marl, and shell, often dusting nearby race fans. This 4.1-mile track operated from 1948 to 1958. (Courtesy of John Gontner.)

AERIAL VIEW OF THE 4.1-MILE ROAD/BEACH RACE TRACK, PONCE INLET, NORTH TURN, 1955. This track operated from 1948 to 1958. Due to the rapid growth of the area, beach racing was eliminated. Many fans feared that racing was finished with the closing of this track. However, a new enclosed speedway was constructed west of Daytona, on International Speedway Boulevard, and modern racing continues today. (Courtesy of John Gontner.)

LOUISE GARDNER-SUMMERLIN AND HER HUSBAND, RUSSELL SUMMERLIN (CENTER), WITH TWO UNIDENTIFIED FRIENDS. Louise was the former owner of Gardner's Seafood Restaurant. After marrying Russ, they operated a restaurant in the former DuBois home on Halifax Drive, and at the boathouse at Eldora. Years ago, special entertainment was provided by Russell at the piano. Most diners remember him wearing a hat as he played the old songs. (Courtesy of Port Orange Historical Trust.)

GARDNER'S SEAFOOD RESTAURANT, HALIFAX DRIVE. Some of the employees seen here (not in order) are Grace Futch, Ruby Tedder, Mullett Eckerson, Odessa Wilson, Miss Kelly, and Mrs. Sparkman. (Courtesy of Port Orange Historical Trust.)

PORT ORANGE, UNITED STATES POST OFFICE, EARLY 1950S. The post office was a community gathering place when the mail arrived daily. The station wagon pictured belonged to Saraphine Gardner. She owned and operated Gardner's Seafood Restaurant at the present-day location of Sweetwater's Restaurant on the Halifax River. (Courtesy of Port Orange Historical Trust.)

VARNER'S/WALGREEN'S DRUG STORE, 1948. It was operated by Tom Varner for several years, and later it was almost completely destroyed by a fire. It eventually met its demise to make way for a new shopping center which still exits today. In its time, it was a modern day drug store with a lunch counter. It was a popular meeting place for local patrons. (Courtesy of Port Orange Historical Trust.)

CARDWELL-MALONEY FUNERAL HOME, 4084 SOUTH HALIFAX DRIVE. This was the first funeral home established in Port Orange. The building was the original home of H.K. DuBois, the town's first physician and mayor. (Courtesy of Port Orange Historical Trust.)

L.T. Sansbury, Principal of Port Orange School for more than 30 Years. Sansbury was an officer in the United States Navy during World War II and was wounded aboard ship in the South Pacific. He was also in the citrus and cattle business until his death. His orange grove was destroyed by a disastrous freeze in the 1950s, and trees were never replanted. He eventually sold his land to a developer for a subdivision. His cow pasture was sold as well, and today is dotted with homes. (Courtesy of Port Orange Historical Trust.)

Port Orange/South Halifax Lion's Club Annual Meeting. The 1981 meeting was held at San Remo Restaurant with Wade Stephenson, district governor, presiding. The South Halifax Lion's Club was chartered in 1951. (Courtesy of Cardwell Family Collection.)

Port Orange Bridge & Dunlawton Ave. Area

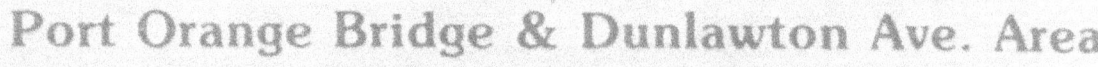

PORT ORANGE BRIDGE, CAUSEWAY, AND SEA BIRD ISLAND. This aerial view shows the Atlantic Ocean, Halifax River, and the surrounding areas. This bridge (the second Port Orange Bridge) was constructed in 1951 and torn down in 1990 to make way for the new high-span bridge that stands today. (Courtesy of Cardwell Family Collection.)

Nine
GROWTH AND THE FUTURE

VOLUSIA COUNTY BOTANICAL GARDENS. The gardens are located on the grounds of the historic Dunlawton Plantation. (Courtesy of Cardwell Family Collection.)

AUNT CATFISH'S, 4009 HALIFAX DRIVE. This is the former site of Dave's Dock and Dave's Dock Restaurant. (Courtesy of Port Orange Historical Trust.)

SWEETWATER'S RESTAURANT, 3633 HALIFAX DRIVE, ON THE RIVER. Originally Gardner's Seafood—one of the area's most outstanding seafood restaurants—Sweetwater's is also the former site of the Sandbar and the Showboat Restaurants. (Courtesy of Port Orange Historical Trust.)

PORT ORANGE BRIDGE, BUILT IN 1990. Pictured is the high-span bridge that is named for, and honors, former Congressman William "Bill" V. Chappell. (Courtesy of Port Orange Historical Trust.)

FIRST BAPTIST CHURCH OF PORT ORANGE, BUILT 1961, 316 CHURCH STREET. This sanctuary stands on the historic site of the original First Baptist Church, 1931. (Courtesy of Port Orange Historical Trust.)

FIRST UNITED METHODIST CHURCH OF PORT ORANGE, BUILT 1963. Located on the southeast corner of Herbert Street and Orange Avenue, this church replaced the old 1906 structure. It was first organized in 1895. (Courtesy of Port Orange Historical Trust.)

THE NEW GRACE EPISCOPAL CHURCH, BUILT 1985, 4110 RIDGEWOOD AVENUE. This sanctuary stands near the old pioneer church, which is a historic landmark for Port Orange. (Courtesy of Port Orange Historical Trust.)

CARDWELL-MALONEY FUNERAL HOME, 3571 RIDGEWOOD AVENUE. This is the second funeral home established by Glen A. Cardwell, LFD (Licensed Funeral Director). (Courtesy of Port Orange Historical Trust.)

PORT ORANGE ELEMENTARY SCHOOL, 402 DUNLAWTON AVENUE. Built in 1925, the school is shown here with two floors and new additions. This photo was taken 1999. (Courtesy of Cardwell Family Collection.)

NEW PORT ORANGE CITY HALL, 1000 CITY CENTER CIRCLE, BUILT IN 1990. This building houses the city government, including the mayor's office, city manager's office, and council chamber. (Courtesy of Port Orange Historical Trust.)

NEW PORT ORANGE REGIONAL LIBRARY, 1005 CITY CENTER CIRCLE. (Courtesy of Port Orange Historical Trust.)

PORT ORANGE FIRE STATION NO. 1. The station is located at 210 Commonwealth Boulevard. (Courtesy of Port Orange Historical Trust.)

PORT ORANGE FIRE STATION NO. 2. Station No. 2 is located at 5839 Trailwood Drive. (Courtesy of Port Orange Historical Trust.)

PORT ORANGE FIRE STATION NO. 3, 1090 CITY CENTER BOULEVARD. This modern station evolved from the early "all-volunteer" department that once was housed near the old city hall, near Dunlawton and Ridgewood Avenues. (Courtesy of Port Orange Historical Trust.)

FIRE STATION NO. 4, 6701 AIRPORT ROAD. The personnel for the city's fire and rescue teams totals 64. (Courtesy of Port Orange Historical Trust.)

CITY OF PORT ORANGE POLICE DEPARTMENT, 1395 DUNLAWTON AVENUE. The previous police department headquarters were at Dunlawton and Ridgewood Avenue. C.J. Vass, marshall, was the first law enforcement officer in 1913 when the town was incorporated. He was later replaced by I.J. Wells Jr. Until formal police protection could be implemented, the sheriff's deputy, constable, or marshall were available to keep law and order in the Port Orange area. Today's staff and officers total 100. (Courtesy of Port Orange Historical Trust.)

THE GOLF CLUB AT CYPRESS HEAD, OWNED BY THE CITY OF PORT ORANGE. The club house and golf course are located at 6231 Palm Vista Street. (Courtesy of Port Orange Historical Trust.)

EDNA MAY CLIFTON. Edna May Clifton was 100 years old when this photo was taken; however, she lived to be 102. She was married to Roy Clifton, who served as police chief and a longtime law enforcement officer in Port Orange. She was outspoken and well versed in civic matters dealing with the City of Port Orange. (Courtesy of Port Orange Historical Trust.)

ELMER AND HIS WIFE, JERRY MCDONALD, AT THE PORT ORANGE SCHOOL REUNION, 1983. Prominent members of the Port Orange Historical Trust, Elmer and Jerry assisted with organizing the Port Orange School Reunion. Jerry was the treasurer for the reunion committee, and Elmer always made sure that the classmates had swamp cabbage on the menu. Elmer was a local cattleman and descendant of the A.E. McDonald family, pioneers that came to the area in 1856. (Courtesy of Port Orange Historical Trust.)

PORT ORANGE/SOUTH HALIFAX LION'S CLUB, 1994–1995. The club dedicated a bronze marker honoring Lion Floy Edgar at the Port Orange Bridge Causeway Gazebo. Edgar was responsible for the beautification of the Port Orange Causeway and many other Lion's projects. Lion Harold D. Cardwell Sr. (front, in vest with emblem) presided over the ceremony. (Courtesy of Cardwell Family Collection.)

LION'S CLUB DEDICATION. In 1993, the South Halifax Lion's Club marker dedicating the Port Orange Causeway was placed in the honor of Floy Edgar, a local concrete products manufacturer, philanthropist, and civic leader. The marker was relocated to the causeway recreational site after the new high-span bridge construction. (Courtesy of Port Orange Historical Trust.)

CARDWELL FAMILY REUNION, JULY 4, 1999. Family members (not listed in order) are Harold and Priscilla Cardwell, H. Douglas and Ann Cardwell, Timmy and Jason Cardwell, Ruth Cardwell-Landau and Glenn Landau, Lindsey Rewis, Chelsea and Dakota Landau, Thelma Cardwell, Barbara Cardwell-Kazebeer, Alexis Goff, and Amanda Boada. (Courtesy of Cardwell Family Collection.)

BATTLE OF DUNLAWTON COMMEMORATION, JANUARY 16, 2000. Pictured from left to right are Dr. Joe Knetsch, Harold D. Cardwell Sr., and Mayor Dorothy Hukill. In the background is the 29-piece Daytona Beach Concert Band that provided special music for the occasion. In addition, the Embry Riddle Aeronautical University Military Cadets presented the colors. (Courtesy of Cardwell Family Collection.)

DUNLAWTON SUGAR MILL AND BOTANICAL GARDENS OF VOLUSIA, INC. Seen from left to right in the foreground are Les Tripp, president; and Martin Wittbold, first vice-president of the Botanical Gardens of Volusia, Inc.; and Harold D. Cardwell Sr., president of the Port Orange Historical Trust. In 1999, this machinery was renovated and protective coating was applied to the mill parts. These improvements were made possible by the Volusia County government. (Courtesy of Port Orange Historical Trust.)

PORT ORANGE HISTORICAL TRUST. Members pictured, from left to right, are Thelma Cardwell, secretary; Harold D. Cardwell Sr., president; Tony Kubacki, director; and Carol Kubacki, treasurer. The Port Orange Historical Trust meets once a month, except for July and August. (Courtesy of Port Orange Historical Trust.)

TOP IMAGE: PORT ORANGE HISTORICAL TRUST, 3431 RIDGEWOOD AVENUE. Members gathered at a recent meeting are, from left to right, Ruth Charles, Robert Charles, Inez Winn, Bonnie Haller, Thelma Cardwell, and Shirley Sheppard. (Courtesy of Port Orange Historical Trust.)

MIDDLE IMAGE: PORT ORANGE HISTORICAL TRUST, MUSEUM AND ARCHIVES. The historic Battle of Dunlawton was fought near this site on January 19, 1836. (Courtesy of Port Orange Historical Trust.)

BOTTOM IMAGE: THE CURRENT HOME OF THE PORT ORANGE HISTORICAL TRUST, 3431 RIDGEWOOD AVENUE. Board member Shirley Sheppard greets Carol Kubacki at a recent gathering of volunteers. (Courtesy of Port Orange Historical Trust.)

www.ingramcontent.com/pod-product-compliance
Lightning Source LLC
Chambersburg PA
CBHW080905100426
42812CB00007B/2169